"Conscious Mind Treatment"

The New Technology of Conscious Mind Treatment

By Dr. Hank Seitz

Creating Worldly Success and Eternal Peace

Conscious Mind Treatment

Author: Dr. Hank Seitz
Managing Editor: Jaime A. Garzaro
Edited by Laura Armbruster of Valuable Connections
Illustrated by Lilian Oliveira of Lumi Creative Studio
Prepared for publication by Jaime A. Garzaro
Published by Guaranteed Measurable Results, LLC
Printed in the United States of America.

For more information and downloads please visit www.ConsciousMindTreatment.com

Guaranteed Measurable Results, LLC

cmt@gmresults.com
www.gmresults.com
1717 Old Course Drive
Plano, TX 75093

ISBN: 1453808760
EAN-13: 9781453808764

This book is dedicated to the Spirit within each one of us.

Table of Contents

Table of Contents 5

Table of Contents

Table of Contents 7

Table of Contents 8

Foreword

This book is written for those seeking eternal Peace and worldly success. For years I was unable to find Peace and Happiness, despite worldly successes for myself and others.

In my search and desire to find worldly prosperity, I have always been disappointed as the future held uncertainty, and ultimately everything in this world goes to dust and death. Once I discovered the Truth, through *Conscious Mind Treatment*, I was able to realize eternal Peace and Happiness.

Throughout the book I refer to our essence using the words such as God, Christ, Spirit, Intelligence, Father, and The Source. Feel free to substitute any of these words for the words that best relate to your understanding of your essence and where you come from. For example, if you are not a Christian, when the word Christ is used consider this to be the Christ Consciousness where you recognize your oneness with your Creator.

No longer must we think we have storms in our Lives. Instead, we can live now with the thought of only a passing cloud upon a sky eternally serene, as we plant our thought in the green lawn of Heaven. This is the essence of *Conscious Mind Treatment*, as our conscious mental focus rises from our lower selves to our Higher Selves...no longer managed by the *"committee."*

It is my hope that this book helps you find your Happiness and Truth, while having prosperity here on earth.

Your Mind is in for a Treat!

Chapter 1

Conscious Mind Treatment and "The Goal"

This book is written for those that seek eternal Peace and Happiness, while seeking success in this world. If you seek to recognize and live in Heaven while experiencing success, this is a path to your inheritance.

Through the years I have been fortunate to find many solutions (some call "secrets") for the success of thousands of people, hundreds of large and small companies and individuals, both professionally and personally. The teachings in this book are time proven techniques and processes that have created wealth of all types for these organizations and individuals. However, this is not only a self-improvement book, but rather a book that will provide you a road to everlasting Happiness, Joy, and Peace.

Many have set goals with me, and using the techniques in this book have achieved their worldly goals and objectives of a more fulfilling and successful Life. This is not the intent of "The Goal" that you can achieve after reading this book, though these same principles can achieve your worldly goals as well. However, you shall find another place that is filled with far greater Gifts than this world can ever offer, and shall last for eternity. There is a means to be in this world, while living in Heaven, and you can experience this for yourself as I have.

After 22 years of formal education, 15 years in training and development with P&G, and 15 years helping organizations enhance their wealth, I have found that none of the worldly goals are everlasting. In fact, the world is changing so fast that one experiences a glimpse of success only to discover more misery. Misery from the workplace, death of a loved one, a relationship gone sour, and a host of other world events that puts one in hell again. A cobweb that we all seem to get caught in, and then ultimately stung as we believe any Good will only last until the next moment.

Many a book or story has been told where the "punch line" is at the end. One such book was "Three Words" that ended with the three words "I am God." This is a glaring statement of blasphemy unless you read the book to understand its meaning. This book shall start with the "punch line" and then share with you how to achieve both "The Goal" and your success in this world using the knowledge of Conscious Mind Treatment.

"The Goal" that rises above all goals is to recognize our Oneness with God. Once we recognize our Oneness with God, all things shall be given to us. We are all one with God, we just do not recognize our

Oneness, as we decided to be separate and create our own Heaven that usually ends up in hell. Attempting to manage this world typically ends in another feeble attempt that puts us aimlessly in a cesspool of guilt, shame, doubt, and uncertainty. Our attempts to find Happiness usually leads us back to the seemingly reliable sorrow and unhappiness, with more to come just around the horizon.

There must be a better way. Are we just here to be born, go to school, get married, have children, and then die? Would God give us such a gloomy destiny that ends in death? No, God has not led us to this world; we led ourselves to this world when we decided we could have something better than Heaven. God gave us choices, and we ended up here. This separation is depicted in the Bible when Adam and Eve chose other than God. Though we appear separated, we shall always be One with God. Our state of consciousness takes us away from this realization, believing that we are our bodies, as we imagine that this world is real. It is real but only based on our own perception as imagined by our smaller self with our small and limited thinking.

As we seek Happiness, we search for the Truth. But what is the Truth? The Truth is that we are made in the image and likeness of God, as Genesis states in the Old Testament. The Truth is that we are not our bodies. As Christ told us to pray the Lord's Prayer, it begins with "Our Father." Not just Christ's Father, with Christ being the only Son of God, and us being just 'children of God.' We all have the same Father, and we are all Sons of God with Christ. The difference between Christ and us is His ability to realize the Truth. As Christ is the Son of God, so must we be the Son of God.

Imagine a large oak tree in the spring. The base of the tree is God, all limbs coming from the base are spiritual leaders of the world, and one such limb is Christ. From each major limb are many branches, the branches representing our "family tree." And from the branches are small budding leaves. We are these leaves, and the tree continues to grow. Are we not part of God, all part of the same tree?

We all come from the same source

1. The Tree is God
2. The Limbs are our Heritage
3. Leaves & Buds are the People

When Christ was in the boat during a storm, the people while engaged in their smaller selves were concerned while Christ peacefully slept. Christ was not concerned with the world. He recognized his Oneness with God and knew that nothing in this world is real but our own perceptions. He knew nothing could hurt Him. If the world were real, we would all perceive it in the same way. But we do not perceive anything exactly the same. Even a death could be sorrow for some, and a time to rejoice for others. 9/11 is a good example of sorrow for us, and rejoicing for Al-Qaeda.

The New Technology of CMT

CMT is the new technology that stands for *Conscious Mind Treatment.* CMT is the method in which you will achieve The Goal of recognizing our Oneness with God. To achieve The Goal we need to change our Conscious Mind through Treatment with the Truth. To begin, simply recognize that we are not our bodies, and that nothing in this world is God's Truth. The world will not bring you Peace and Happiness for eternity. There is a better way and that way is to think differently than our current state of consciousness. If not, we shall continue to live in unhappiness and uncertainty. As we understand the Truth we shall be set free...let our freedom ring and Peace be ours. Though some believe there are 7 or 8 habits, there is only one habit to know - the habit of recognizing our Oneness with God and each other.

As we change and treat our thinking and conscious mind, we shall live in eternal Peace, Joy, and Happiness right now. We already have everything we need once we understand the Truth and are led by the Holy Spirit. The balance of this book will treat your conscious mind and you will be led to do God's Will. No longer will you be deceived by **f.e.a.r.** (**f**alse **e**vidence **a**ppearing **r**eal), death, pain, loss, and loneliness. Your eyes will be open to see at last, as God's gentle correction will have you see your present and eternal Happiness.

Chapter 2

The Red Zones We Live In

CMT starts with understanding where we are and the areas in which we live. There are three zones of our Lives where we find ourselves living, where our smaller self (our ego) attempts to run the Life to our demise. The only devil there is are these three red zones that we have chosen to live in. Consider each of these zones and reflect on how you find yourself living in the red, or living in hell, during your day and Life.

Doing Important Things Urgently
Red Zone One

The first red zone is where we are doing important things, urgently. Whenever we are in the midst of urgency, we are guided by our smaller self. How many times have we risen in the morning and had a plan of action only to find our plan crumbling before our eyes as other people changed it? Or, we had a plan for our work day with all the things we wanted to accomplish, and by the end of the day we were exhausted and recognized that we accomplished little of our initial plan. Not only do other people manage our Life, consider how your own thoughts prevent you from living in grace and experiencing a peaceful and fulfilling day. This zone is where "Life Manages Me!"

This same situation is found in our personal Lives. On Friday night we have a list of things we would like to do for the weekend.   This list may include being intentional and investing time with loved ones, or cleaning out a closet, or paying bills. Saturday morning you awake and you are asked to run an errand, then work on some project of another's, and then run someone else's errand. During the day you think ill thoughts about something or someone. Before you know it, Saturday afternoon is upon you and your list has been untouched. You have done some important things like making breakfast, cleaning up, and taking the kids to a ball game, but few of the things YOU wanted to achieve.

By Sunday night we say to ourselves "Where did the weekend go?" as few of the things we wanted to achieve in our personal lives are accomplished. We are reactive to Life, doing other important things, but not the things on our list that we wanted to do! We end up by the end of the weekend, or end of the work day, frustrated, stressed out, with a feeling of bondage and lack of control of our Lives. Yet, we are unaware that nothing can hurt us but our own thoughts. Indeed, this red zone has the smell of hell in the air. The net result finds us in a state that lacks success and most certainly increases our stress.

The Areas We Live In - Red Zone 1

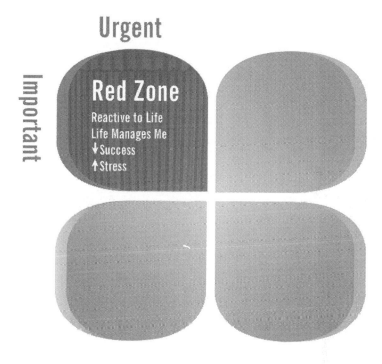

Doing Non-Important Things Urgently
Red Zone Two

We also find ourselves doing non-important things, and doing them urgently, placing us in another red zone. This zone includes "busy work" where we do everything but what we set out to do. For example, Saturday morning you awake and have some coffee, read the paper, then turn on the TV, and before you know it Saturday afternoon is upon you and your objectives have been untouched. Your stress increases. As you look back on the day, you realize that it lacked accomplishment because you were emerged in *"low pay off activities."*

You may have a plan each day of what you would like to achieve at work. You get into work and soon someone interrupts you and asks for you to do something for them. Your email box is filled with one request after the next, you check your snail mail, receive too many phone calls, and think about unimportant things and your little self as you find that your day was consumed with "busy work." Little was achieved that would help you become more successful.

The Areas We Live In – Red Zone 2

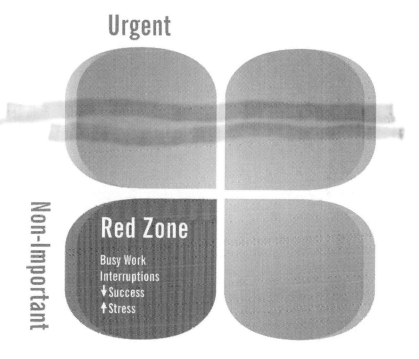

Doing Non-Important Things Non-Urgently
Red Zone Three

When we are engaged in doing non-important things, and doing them non-urgently, we are in another red zone. This is where the *"committee"* resides. The *"committee"* is that voice that tells us things like "how could I have done that?", "why did I say that?" and a host of other negative and judgmental thoughts.

Through the years we have been told not to talk to ourselves, yet we all talk to ourselves all the time! Laughter creates positive endorphins that are healthier for you than any drug known to man. The *"committee"* creates negative endorphins, the most poisonous drug known to man, creating a call for inaction or negative action, and a compromise of who you really are.

The *"committee"* consists of many players, each of them fighting for your demise. One of the main *"committee"* members is f.e.a.r., an acronym that stands for **F**alse **E**vidence **A**ppearing **R**eal. The insurance industry was concerned over the number of people dying and the need to pay the so-called Life Insurance policies (though they are death insurance policies!). They found that the number one cause of death was heart disease, and that heart disease was caused by stress. They found that stress was primarily caused by our own thoughts of f.e.a.r., and that 93% of the things we fear never happen to us!

Thus was born the phrase false evidence appearing real.

Our mind initiates and creates everything. When we waste our thoughts with *"committee"* members, we are wasting our Lives and walking a path to our destruction. In addition to f.e.a.r., other *"committee"* members include worry, doubt (the opposite of faith), complaining, blaming (a call for inaction), guilt, revenge, attack, and shame. All these *"committee"* member thoughts lead to our unhappiness, lack of success, and increased stress. As our stress results from our f.e.a.r., and that leads to heart disease, the *"committee"* can actually lead you to your death! In fact, the *"committee"* unfortunately rejoices in your death.

Of the three, we spend most of our time in this red zone, thinking and creating ill will for ourselves and others with that damn *"committee."* In religious terms, the *"committee"* is the devil. It states not who we really are and creates hell right here on earth. The only power the *"committee"* has is what we give it. The *"committee"* is powerless without your support and belief in the insane ideas it comes up with. I had one client who not only recognized her *"committee,"* but confessed that she had many board rooms filled with different *"committees"* with many *"committee"* members in each one!

To control the *"committee"* is to control your Life and live in Heaven right here on earth. To do this you need only to observe your thoughts and accept only those that are for your greater good. There is your lower self and Higher Self, as recognized when one says "I said to myself" implying that there are two entities here, the "I" and the "myself." Raise your right hand and point back to yourself. The "I" is your Higher Self observing you with your hand as you look in and observe your lower self, or the "myself." As you observe your thoughts, choose only those that are positive and support your goals and dreams while recognizing your oneness with God. You are in control of your destiny only by the thoughts you choose.

The "committee" provides all the negative thoughts that you could ever want. It has conditioned you to take the "easy" path, or so it appears, while it is in control of the demise of your Life. The chairperson of the board is the Judge who asks questions such as "why did I say that?" and "why did I do that?" along with our thoughts of self-criticism, doubt, and ultimate destruction of knowing your True and Higher Self. When you think with your "committee," you judge all. This judgment from your small self declares how you will perceive your world. Your perception and what you see with your physical eyes originates from your thoughts. Committee thoughts will have you see a mean and cruel world. Your Higher Self will see the world as Christ does - filled only with Love.

Your mind is like a river running through your head. The river represents your thoughts, and your mind is always thinking even when you are sleeping. Now sit your Higher Self on the bank of the river and watch your thoughts go by, choosing only those that are for your Peace, Joy, Happiness, and success!

The Areas We Live In – Red Zone 3

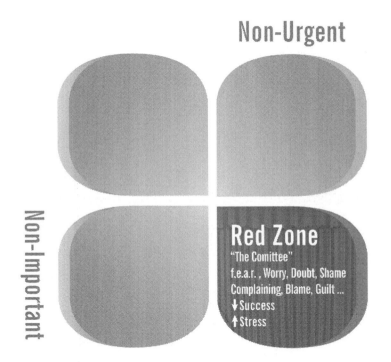

Non-Urgent

Non-Important

Red Zone
"The Comittee"
f.e.a.r. , Worry, Doubt, Shame
Complaining, Blame, Guilt ...
↓ Success
↑ Stress

Chapter 3

Living In The "Green Zone"

The *"Green Zone"* is where you are led by your Teacher or the Holy Spirit. The Holy Spirit is always communicating and guiding you. It is up to you to be intentional and have your mind STILL to listen and be directed by the Holy Spirit. This is where you are intentional, pro-active, and where "I Manage Life"! These words provide a sweet smell of triumph as we manage our Life.

We have created in our minds a red curtain of f.e.a.r. that hides our true essence. Behind this red curtain of f.e.a.r. lie all the Peace, Happiness, and Joy that we have always deserved. Behind this red curtain rests God waiting for you to come Home. As we let go of illusions that are caused by f.e.a.r., what awaits us is the Shining welcome and our return to Love in our minds. We lay down our false perceptions and images that we have worshipped, now a mere shadow that only requires Light to have them dissipate. Only the Truth and Love remains as the Light of God is revealed.

Wherever we are in our Life can be called Point A. Where we want to go is Point B. Our intention is to stay on the line from point A to point B as we identify specific action steps and track our daily thoughts and behaviors. As you dismiss the *"committee"* you enter point B, or heaven here on earth, as depicted on the *"Point A to Point B Graph"*. If you allow the *"committee"* to rule your thoughts, with words like: "I can't do that.", "I'm too slow, dumb, or whatever", you shall be in a mental state called *"hell"*!

Point A To Point B Graph

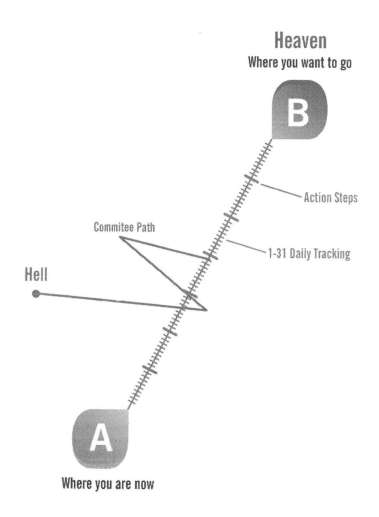

The Areas We Live In – The Green Zone

Urgent   Non-Urgent

Important

Red Zone

Reactive to Life
Life Manages Me
↓Success
↑Stress

Green Zone

Being Intentional, Pro-Active
I Manage Life, Spirit
↑Success
↓Stress

Non-Important

Red Zone

Busy Work
Interruptions
↓Success
↑Stress

Red Zone

"The Comittee "
f.e.a.r., Worry, Doubt, Shame
Complaining, Blame, Guilt ...
↓Success
↑Stress

If you don't manage your Life...someone else will! Your Happiness and success depends upon your intention and how you plan to be. To be intentional is to leave the red zones, particularly the "*committee*," and to think and do important things non-urgently. Your destiny depends upon your thoughts at this moment. Let us now plant seeds in our mind that will sow more success and less stress in your Life, both personally and professionally. The planting of good seeds, as led by the Holy Spirit, is the essence of *Conscious Mind Treatment.*

The first seed is to know that if you continue to do the things that you have always done, you will continue to get what you have always gotten. The first step to live in the green zone is to be led by the Holy Spirit to change our thinking from that of the world to that of God's thought. You will be guided on what you should be and achieve, with all the right thoughts, words, and deeds.

The most cherished goal one can have is to achieve his recognition of being one with God. This goal is the only eternal and everlasting goal and it lies beyond this world. It is also the only goal that will bring true Peace, Happiness, and Joy to you. We will use the *"The God Goal Planning Sheet"* to guide us to our Happiness. The suggested stated God goal would be "To Recognize My Oneness With God." Your benefits could include "Eternal Peace," "Eternal Happiness," "Eternal Joy," and "Living In Heaven." Your losses to avoid might be "Avoid Living In Hell Here On Earth," "Dying and Going To Hell," and then the opposite of your benefits that could include not experiencing Peace, Happiness, and Joy.

Your goal can be achieved instantly or take as long as you think it will take as you are in control. However, since most of us are so emerged in this world and its changing truths, "The God Goal" development is likely required. Your action steps to recognize your oneness with God could include the following:

- ✓ To be still and think about God each morning for 10 minutes.

- ✓ To be still and think about God each evening for 10 minutes prior to going to bed.

- ✓ To read a spiritual book such as the Bible, "Conversations With God," or "A Course In Miracles."

- ✓ Read a daily devotional book.

- ✓ Meditate each day, still your mind, quiet thyself, quiet your "committee," and be with your Higher Self.

- ✓ Listen and feel God's presence.

Whenever you have a question on what to think, say, or do, ask the Holy Spirit. Ask only for all of God's Holy Thoughts to surround you.

These action steps can then be tracked on the *1-31 Tracking Sheet*, which we will discuss later in this chapter.   These action steps and tracking tool will help you to stay focused in the Green Zone, away from the red zones, and will treat your Mind to think Godly thoughts. Within seconds, days, or weeks you shall receive guidance and recognize your oneness with God. The amount of time it takes depends on your Belief.

Your God Goal Planning Sheet

Goal:

To recognize my oneness with God.

Personal Benefits:

1. Eternal Peace
2. Eternal Happiness
3. Eternal Joy
4. Living In Heaven
5. Less Anxiety
6. Less Negative Thoughts that bring me down
7. Less Sleeping
8.

Action Steps:

1. To be still for 10 minutes every morning
2.   and think about God.
3. To be still and think about God for 10 minutes
4. To read a spiritual book every evening.
5. Listen and feel God's presence
6.
7.
8.
9.
10.

Since we invest more conscious hours in our professional Life, we will now identify our goals at work. Your professional goal should measure your current level of productivity, what you are currently achieving every day, month, and/or project. Consider your professional goal and ensure it meets the S.M.A.R.T. (Specific, Measurable, Achievable, Realistic, and Time-framed) and productive criteria, then write your goal on the *"Professional Goal Planning Sheet."*

Your Professional Goal Planning Sheet

Goal:

To get a suitable PT job.

Personal Benefits:

1. higher self-esteem
2. more money
3. happier home life
4. less stress
5. creative outlet good for me
6.
7.
8.

Action Steps:

1. Go to craig's list
2. Enter a writing contest.
3. Write about something and try to sell it
4. Try writing a song.
5.
6.
7.
8.
9.
10.

Your current level of professional productivity is referred to as our starting point or "A." Where you are led to go and do God's Will is referred to as "B." We only do things for two reasons - to gain a personal benefit or avoid a personal loss. Personal benefits could include higher self-esteem, more money, enhanced career opportunities, less stress, and a happier home Life as your job typically affects your behavior at home. Consider now why you will benefit by achieving your professional goal and write it down on the Goal Planning Sheet.

Your "High and Low Pay Off Activities"

Identify your "*High Pay Off Activities*," those thoughts and behaviors that are most important and add value and achievement to your Life. The first "*HPOA*" is to be led by the Holy Spirit and then plan the steps to achieve your goal. Planning starts with your goals that are led by Spirit where you use your Goal Planning Sheet and write down your goal, your personal benefits, and specific action steps to achieve your goal.

Based on your goals and *High Pay Off Activities*, you will then plan your month, week, and each day. At the end of each month plan your next month by using a calendar and writing down the intentional activities you will take for the month. This may include the days you will exercise, the days and times you will invest with loved ones, and the time you will devote to projects that lead to your success. On Sunday night, plan your week and write down what day and time you will do your success activities. The night before each coming day, plan out time slots where you will be engaged in the thoughts and activities that support your goal.

We think we know what we do each day, but the *"committee"* deceives us and we move into doing *"Low Pay Off Activities"* in the red zones. What we see in Life reflects only the process in our mind. Our small ideas start the process where we make up what the smaller mind desires, judges to be valuable, and seek to find. These images in our smaller mind are then projected outward and seen as real and guarded as one's own. This process leads to a perception of a damned world where we live in hell. To become conscious of your smaller mind's thoughts and then activities, record your activities for three days, every fifteen minutes. Most of us are only engaged in *High Pay Off Activities* 30% of the time, and your tracking of *LPOA's* will help you determine the thoughts and behaviors that require changing.

Tracking High Pay Off Activities Sheet

List your high pay off activities in the first vertical columns, then begin to list your low pay off activities as they occur during the day in the LPOA's vertical columns. Indicate how much time you spend, in fifteen minute intervals, during the day in both your HPOA's and LPOA's

	HPOA's					LPOA's			
6:00am									
6:15am									
6:30am									
6:45am									
7:00am									
7:15am									
7:30am									
7:45am									
8:00am									
8:15am									
8:30am									
8:45am									
9:00am									
9:15am									
9:30am									
9:45am									
10:00am									
10:15am									
10:30am									
10:45am									
11:00am									
11:15am									
11:30am									
11:45am									
12:00pm									
12:15pm									
12:30pm									
12:45pm									
1:00pm									
1:15pm									
1:30pm									
1:45pm									
2:00pm									
2:15pm									
2:30pm									
2:45pm									
3:00pm									
3:15pm									
3:30pm									
3:45pm									
4:00pm									
4:15pm									
4:30pm									
4:45pm									
5:00pm									

Your Higher Self can be awakened and attainment of your goals secured as you take control of your destiny. Here is how:

✓ Ask the Holy Spirit to help you determine your goals to ensure everlasting Happiness and Peace.

✓ Identify what you want to be/do/achieve in your professional and personal Life.

✓ Observe your thoughts, and choose only positive thoughts that will lead you to the achievement of your goals.

✓ Identify what your *"High Pay Off Activities"* are in both your professional and personal Life. These are the activities that are most critical to your success.

✓ Plan your month, week, and day.

✓ Track Your Progress Using The *1-31 Tracking Sheet*

The only moment you control is the Present Moment. The past is dead and distorted, the future unknown, and all the power we have is right now! That power right now is your Present Moment thoughts and daily habits. Ultimately you will experience Holy Instants each present moment as you treat your mind. Many of our daily habits aren't necessarily successful habits. The *1-31 Tracking Sheet* is an effective tool to first identify your new thoughts and behaviors, and then implement them for our success.

The first professional behavior to track is your daily planning. At the end of each day a check mark is put when you plan your day, and a dash mark if you neglect your daily planning. Other behaviors and *"High Pay Off Activities"* are identified that support your goals and tracked using the *1-31 Tracking Sheet.* For example, if you are a sales representative, daily behaviors to track could be the number of referrals you receive per week, the number of sales presentations per week, and the number of closes per month. Daily planning would also include planning your personal Life that includes Saturday, Sunday, vacation days, and holidays. Begin to plan the night before, regardless of whether it is a work day or personal day.

Under the *"Personal Goals"* tracking, the first daily behavior to track is thinking about God each morning with prayer, devotions, or meditation. Contemplate how you are one with God and remember who you really are. Your essence is not of this world and your contemplation will help you remember that you are the Son of God, sinless, and directed by Spirit. Sit quietly, be STILL, and have God communicate with you. This exercise should be done both in the morning and at night.

The *1-31 Tracking Sheet* can be made on a spreadsheet and should be placed on your refrigerator, carried with you, or saved in your computer. A hard copy is preferred and should be visible to you as a reminder to track your daily behaviors. Recently a client of mine identified the following items to track on their *1-31 Tracking Sheet*:

   ✓ Plan each day the night before.

   ✓ Intentional Breathing while stating the affirmation "I am decisive" 100 times per day.

   ✓ One extraordinary act of affection to my spouse each day.

   ✓ Be STILL and make Peace with the Present Moment!

1-31 Day Tracking Sheet

Personal Goals

	1	2	3	4	5	6	7	8	9	10	11	12	13	14	15	16	17	18	19	20	21	22	23	24	25	26	27	28	29	30	31
Think of God 2X/day																															

Business Goals

	1	2	3	4	5	6	7	8	9	10	11	12	13	14	15	16	17	18	19	20	21	22	23	24	25	26	27	28	29	30	31
Plan every day																															

Developing Your Personal Goal

Conscious Mind Treatment includes a balanced personal and professional Life that is essential to your success, with your key focus on God and being led by the Holy Spirit. We are usually clearer on what we are going to achieve in our professional Life, and let our personal Life unfold as it may. This approach often gives us a Life filled with unhappiness, stress, and lack of success. Consider now what you would like to achieve in your personal Life by looking at the areas of your *"Wheel of Life."* Use the *"Wheel of Life"* graph and put a dash mark on each spoke of your Life where you believe you rank. There are 10 marks on each spoke, from lowest (closest to the center) to highest (the outside of the wheel). The areas of your Life to consider are:

Educational: What are you doing to fill your mind with good and positive ideas? How are you growing with your knowledge? Are you taking any educational courses? How often do you read? Do you read spiritual material?

Health: Consider your weight management, diet, exercise, hydration (water intake), meditation/prayer, recreation, stress management, and any unhealthy habits you wish to end.

Social: How socially active are you? Do you belong to a charity or organization that helps others? Are you a good neighbor? Do you honor other people?

Do you pray for others? Do you shed your Light of Love on others?

Spiritual: Do you invest time with God each morning and night? Do you pray? Do you meditate? How honest are you with yourself and others?

Family & Loved Ones: Do you plan one-on-one time with each family member daily or weekly? Do you plan your week each Sunday with your family? How is your Love relationship with your significant other? How is your relationship with your children and/or relatives?

Financial & Career: Do you have an investment plan for your retirement? Have you considered strategies to build your personal wealth? Do you have a vision for your career? Do you have written goals with specific action steps with your job?

Wheel of Life

After reviewing your *"Wheel of Life,"* consider what area of your Life you are most interested in improving. Then develop your personal goal and make sure that it is a S.M.A.R.T. goal, being **S**pecific, **M**easurable, **A**ttainable, **R**ealistic, and **T**ime-framed. If the goal is not measurable, ensure that your action steps are measureable. For example, if you choose a goal "To become healthier," your action steps should include measurables such as the number of times a week you exercise, how much water you drink each day, your daily diet intake of specific foods or vitamins, and other daily behaviors that will lead you to greater health. Now write your personal goal in the "Goal Planning Sheet," the benefits you will achieve from the attainment of the goal, along with several action steps that you will take to begin your journey of success. Your action steps should initially be easy and manageable steps, baby steps that will lead you to achieving your goal.

Your Personal Goal Planning Sheet

Goal:

_____

_____

Personal Benefits:

1. _____
2. _____
3. _____
4. _____
5. _____
6. _____
7. _____
8. _____

Action Steps:

1. _____
2. _____
3. _____
4. _____
5. _____
6. _____
7. _____
8. _____
9. _____
10. _____

Chapter 4

Understanding Yourself and Others

CMT looks upon our fellow man from a different perspective. By understanding the Behaviors and Values of yourself and others, we will look at them with empathy, understanding, and Love.

The Four Behavioral Styles

In 400 B.C., Hippocrates identified four major behavioral styles that humans possess. In the past 100 years much research has been conducted to validate these behavioral styles. In the past few years, technology has fine-tuned these behaviors into a science, using the acronym D.I.S.C.

Your increased success and ability to build stronger relationships include understanding how to *identify* these behavioral styles in others, and then *modifying* your behavior to ensure more effective communication. We all have a shade we either raise up when we like someone, or draw down if we don't.

Your success will depend on your mental focus that raises up the shade with others to open the door of communication.

The four *Behavioral Styles* are:

The Driver

The first behavioral style is the D, which stands for Driver or Dominant. You can identify a Driver by their tendency to control and demand. 18% of the population has a predominant Driver behavioral style and their predominant emotion is anger. Their expertise includes making decisions, and they will make quick decisions, right or wrong. The key to your success and effective communication with a Driver is to modify your behavior and *be efficient* when speaking to them. Drivers are looking for results and efficiency, and are focused on "how do I handle problems."

Many would judge the Driver as being rough, tough, and too aggressive. We can now look upon this type of person with understanding and recognize that he is merely a Driver. Judgment leaves, acceptance takes its place, and as you modify your Behavior and become more efficient, your relationship will blossom with the Driver.

The Influencer

The I stands for Influencer. You can identify Influencers by their tendency to be outgoing. Influencers typically use many gestures and hand movements while talking. 28% of the population has a predominant Influencer style and their emotion is optimism. Their expertise is in the ability to influence people and usually make good sales people. You would modify your behavior and *become stimulating* when communicating with them. Influencers are looking for the experience and personal approval. They are focused on "how do I influence people."

Many would judge the Influencer as being a talkaholic - too loud and too emotional. We can now look at this type of person with understanding and recognize he is merely an Influencer. Judgment leaves, acceptance takes its place, and as you modify your Behavior and become more stimulating, your relationship will blossom with the Influencer.

The Steady

The S stands for Steady. You can identify a Steady by their tendency to not rock the boat. They typically don't want drastic change and are great team players. They are very concerned with the effect on other people and their expertise lies in their even pace. 40% of the population are Steadys, and their emotion is trust. The key to communication with a Steady is to *be agreeable*. This means don't say the word "no" or "but" to a Steady, otherwise you will lower their shade of communication. Instead, use the word "and" which means you agree with them and simply want to add more value to the discussion. Steadiness people are looking for personal security, and are focused on "how do I handle the pace."

Many would judge the Steady as being introverted with lack of initial commitment to most things as well as not very fun to be around. We can now look upon this type of person with understanding and recognize that he is merely a Steady. Judgment leaves, acceptance takes its place, and as you modify your Behavior and become more agreeable, your relationship will blossom with the Steady.

The Compliant

The C stands for Compliant or Conscientious. You can identify Compliants by their need to know information and their quiet nature. They are interested in facts and data. Their expertise lies in their ability to follow rules and regulations. Only 14% of the population are predominantly Compliant, and their emotion is fear. The key to effective communication with a Compliant is to *be accurate*. "C" people are looking for information to be right. They are focused on "how do I handle rules and regulations."

Many would judge the Conscientious as being a fuddy-duddy nerd, with little personality and not very fun to be around. We can now look upon this type of person with understanding and recognize that he is merely a Conscientious. Judgment leaves, acceptance takes its place, and as you modify your Behavior and become more accurate, your relationship will blossom with the Conscientious.

Behavioral Similarities

The Driver and Influencer are typically extroverted, while the Steady and Compliant are generally introverted. People that are more of a Driver and Compliant are more interested in tasks, while the Influencer and Steady are more interested in relationships. For example, if a married couple has a wife that is a Steady and Influencer, she will be more interested in the relationships, whereas if the husband is a Driver and Compliant, he will be more interested in the required tasks. If they go on vacation, she wants to know who is coming with them, while the husband would be more interested in when they leave, where they are staying, and when they get back. The wife could attempt for a life-time to make the husband warm and fuzzy to no avail. The husband is more concerned with the tasks and is unlikely to become warm and fuzzy!

The 4 D.I.S.C. Behavioral Styles

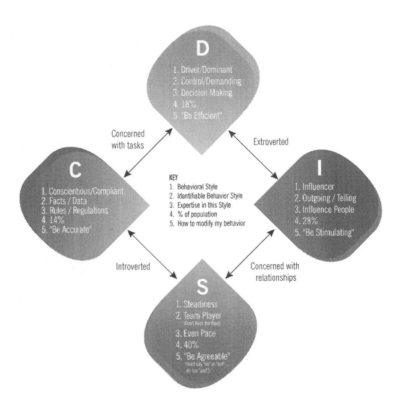

All Behavioral Styles Required

We need all four behaviors to make the world go around and to be balanced. By understanding these different behaviors, we can begin to value and honor each person we meet, without judgment, and with a greater appreciation of our behavioral differences. Your conscious mind will now appreciate our worldly differences, while recognizing that our spirits all come from the same Source and we are One together.

The analogy of the four behavioral styles is: The Driver says "let's charge up this mountain." The Influencer rallies the people and says "we can make it up this mountain faster than anyone." The Steady says "look here D and I, when we go straight up the mountain we will have casualties. Why don't we take the roads that lead up to the top of the mountain?" And finally the C says "look here D, I, and S, when you get to the top of the mountain, you will find that you are on the wrong mountain!" Here lies the value of understanding and modifying our behaviors with all four behavioral styles.

The Six Values of Mankind

Humans have six different values that influence our decision, determine the way we interpret Life, and provide us motivation. By understanding these Values, we can use CMT to enrich our understanding of other people's perspective and can easily "be that other person." We each see Life through a different set of glasses, dependent on the level of our belief based on the six values of mankind below:

Theoretical – This value has to do with the Love of knowledge and truth. This person would surf the net for hours and not accomplish anything other than soaking up knowledge.

Utilitarian – This person values a return on their investment (ROI). This can be a return on their time, energy, money, or any resource that is useful.

Social – This person values helping other people. If this value is high, the person may help others over and above helping themselves!

Traditional – This person is looking for the higher meaning to Life. This could also relate to a strong Judeo-Christian belief or system for living under.

Individualistic – This person is looking for power and can be characteristic of leaders in many fields. They value personal power, influence, and fame. This value does not imply these people are selfish, rather they simply want to be the best.

Aesthetic – This person values form and harmony in Life. Each experience is judged from the standpoint of symmetry, grace, or fitness. This does not necessarily mean he likes to attend art shows, but rather indicates an interest in the artistic aspects of Life.

The Impact of Our Values

Your top two values primarily influence how you make decisions and what motivates you. If your top values are strong, you may not understand why all people don't believe as you do. On the other hand, if you find any of these values hold little interest, you may not understand why a person would have such a value, motivation, or decision-making process.

By understanding the six values of yourself and others, you can better understand the perspective that everyone comes from and embraces a new consciousness of CMT. This is one reason we cannot judge, nor should we judge, other people. We are all diverse and a special perspective is dependent upon our values.

For example, if there were six people on a bus looking at a field of roses, they would all see this same field differently depending upon their values. It is as though there are six windows in the bus, with each person valuing the same field of roses differently. Consider how one might look at a field of roses, dependent on their values:

Theoretical – They view the field of roses and wonder how one grows large roses or colored roses.

Utilitarian – They would be interested in how much they could sell the roses for!

Social – They would want to have other people see the beautiful field of roses, or give them away to a charity.

Traditional – They might look at the field of roses and perceive the stem standing for the growth of Life, with the thorns standing for the challenges in Life, and the flower is the fruit of Life.

Individualistic – They would be motivated in growing the largest rose nursery in the world.

Aesthetic – They might see the field of roses and focus on how each rose color is planted together and in perfect rows.

The *Motivational/Values Graph* indicates the population mean for each of the six values/motivators:

Motivational / Values Graph

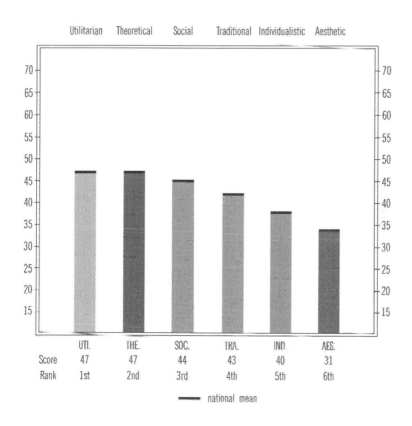

	Utilitarian	Theoretical	Social	Traditional	Individualistic	Aesthetic
	UTI.	THE.	SOC.	TRA.	IND.	AES.
Score	47	47	44	43	40	31
Rank	1st	2nd	3rd	4th	5th	6th

■■■■ national mean

Communicating With Style and Values

Clarity of consciousness enhances your empathy with others, and effective communication is achieved by first understanding your own behavioral style and motivation/values. We can recognize the Behavioral Styles and Motivation/Values of others by observing their behaviors and listening to what their values are.

Most people talk at the rate of about 125 words per minute, while we are thinking between 400 and 600 words per minute. The question is "what are you doing with the extra time?" Are you observing and listening to the other person or are you "out of the room" thinking about what the "committee" wants you to think about?

Living in the *GREEN zone*, and embracing a *Conscious Mind Treatment* includes observing behavior and listening to what motivation and/or values others are expressing. As you modify your behavior to reflect theirs, and speak to their values not your own, you open the window of communication with your fellow sister and brother.

Chapter 5

"The Talents of Mankind"

A man by the name of Dr. Hartman was well educated with a PhD in Mathematics and a law degree. He lived in a major city where he was a well-respected judge. There was a regime that had started in the city and he was quite outspoken on not supporting them. One night Dr. Hartman was at his home with a friend when there was a knock on the door. The person at the door was a friend of Dr. Hartman and reported that some of the Regime's top aides were going to come over and encourage him to support the regime.

Dr. Hartman did not trust the regime and informed his friend that he was leaving his home and would not speak to these aides. The friend stayed at his home and twenty minutes later there was a knock on the door. His friend opened the door and was shot in the head and left to die. The regime was led by Adolph Hitler and these were his aides who assassinated his friend in the city of Berlin.

Shortly after this tragedy Dr. Hartman was reading the Bible and came across a passage regarding the "Talents" of mankind. He had witnessed the greatest evil that man has ever created and now realized that he could create good by understanding the greatest good of man's talents. Dr. Hartman dedicated the rest of his Life in understanding what the talents of mankind were and how to measure them with his background in mathematics. In the 1960's he was nominated for the Nobel Peace Prize as he developed the world's most statistically accurate and valid diagnostic tool to measure man's talents. This diagnostic tool is available at www.consciousmindtreatment.com

There are 67 talents or skills of mankind. We were all born with seeds for each of these talents and during time and experience we have grown some of our talents. All of us have relatively high and low talent rankings, with our higher talents coming from both our experience and those talents that come naturally to us.

The good news is that we can all improve our talents but one must be aware of what mankind's talents are and then develop a plan of action to improve those talents that you choose. Review the talents and definitions of these 67 talents below and select three talents that you would like to improve.

*Accountability for Others – being responsible for the consequences of the actions of those whom you manage.

Attention to Detail – the ability to see and pay attention to details; the ability to recognize the component parts of a procedure or object, and to verify the correctness or error in an individual part or procedure.

Attitude Toward Others – maintaining a positive, open, and objective attitude toward others.

Balanced Decision Making – the ability to be objective and to fairly evaluate the different aspects of a situation, and to make an ethical decision that takes into account all aspects and components; the ability to maintain balance between the needs of oneself, others, and the company at the same time.

*Conceptual Thinking** – the ability to identify and evaluate resources and plan for their utilization throughout the execution of comprehensive, long-range plans.

Concrete Organization – the ability to understand the immediate, concrete needs of a situation and to establish an effective action plan for meeting those needs.

*Conflict Management** – the ability to resolve different points of view constructively.

Consistency and Reliability – the capacity to feel an internal motivation to be conscientious in personal or professional efforts; the need to be consistent and reliable in life roles.

*Continuous Learning** – the ability to take personal responsibility and action toward learning and implementing new ideas, methods and technologies.

Correcting Others – the ability to confront controversial or difficult issues in an objective manner; the ability to have non-emotion discussions about disciplinary matters.

*Customer Focus – A commitment to customer satisfaction.

*Decision Making – The ability to analyze all aspects of a situation to gain thorough insight to make decisions.

*Developing Others – the ability to understand the needs, interests, strengths, and weaknesses of others, and to utilize this information for contributing to the growth and development of others.

*Diplomacy and Tact – the ability to treat others fairly, regardless of personal preferences.

Emotional Control – the ability to maintain a rational and objective demeanor when faced with stressful or emotional situations; a measure of self-composure in a difficult situation and the ability to act objectively, rather than impulsively or emotionally.

*Empathetic Outlook – the ability to perceive and understand the feelings and attitudes of others; the ability to place oneself "in the shoes" of another and to view a situation from their perspective.

Enjoyment of the Job – the feeling that one's job is both fulfilling and rewarding and that it has a positive and useful benefit.

Evaluating Others – the ability to make realistic and accurate judgments about others, to evaluate their strengths and weaknesses, and to understand their manner of thinking, acting, and behaving.

Evaluating What Is Said – a person's openness to people and willingness to hear what other people are saying and not what they think they should say or are going to say.

*Flexibility – the ability to readily modify, respond to, and integrate change with minimal personal resistance.

Following Directions – the ability to effectively hear, understand, and follow directions or instructions; the willingness to postpone making personal decisions, or taking action, until you have openly listened to what you are being asked to do.

Freedom from Prejudice – the ability to not allow unfair implications of prejudged information to enter into and effect an interpersonal relationship; not allowing a person's class, race, sex, ethnicity, or personal philosophy to cause you to prejudge the actions, potential, intentions, or attitudes of others.

Gaining Commitment – the ability to develop and invoke a self-starting attitude in employees in their pursuit of goals; the ability to motivate employees to do their best and to provide them with practical, concrete ideas and methods by which they can achieve their goals.

*Goal Achievement – the overall ability to set, pursue and attain achievable goals, regardless of obstacles or circumstances.

Handling Rejection – the ability to handle rejection on a personal level, based solely on your self-esteem; the ability to see yourself as valuable, separate, and apart from your role or position in life.

Handling Stress – the ability to balance and defuse inner tensions and stresses; the ability to appropriately separate yourself from stressful situations and maintain your own sense of inner peace.

*Influencing Others – the ability to personally affect others' actions, decisions, opinions or thinking.

Initiative – the ability to direct one's energies toward the completion of a goal, without an external catalyst; the ability to initiate actions based on one's own interpretation or understanding of a situation.

Integrative Ability – the ability to identify the elements of a problem situation and understand which components are critical; the ability to see different types of situation structures and therefore, different types of solutions.

Internal Self Control – the ability to maintain rational and objective actions when faced with a stressful and emotional situation.

*Interpersonal Skills – the ability to interact with others in a positive manner.

Intuitive Decision Making – the ability to accurately compile intuitive perceptions about a situation into a decision or action; ability to be 'intuitional' as opposed to intellectual in decision making, and to be effective in doing it.

Job Ethic – the personal commitment an individual makes to executing a specific task.

*Leading Others – the ability to organize and motivate people to get things accomplished in a way that everyone feels a sense of order and direction.

Long Range Planning – the ability to identify long-range goals and design realistic plans to attain them; the ability to see the big picture and then determine what direction to take and how to use resources to attain future goals.

Material Possessions – the ability to recognize the value of material goods.

Meeting Standards – the ability to see and understand the stated requirements established for a job, and a person's commitment to meeting them.

Monitoring Others – the ability to focus on the actions and decisions of others in a practical way to identify both successes and mistakes; the ability to identify the causes of success and failure and to do so in an objective and accurate manner.

*Objective Listening – the ability to listen to many points of view without bias.

Persistence – the ability to stay the course in times of difficulty; the ability to remain motivated to accomplish goals in the face of adversity or obstacles.

*Personal Accountability – the ability to be responsible for the consequences of one's own actions and decisions; taking responsibility for these decisions and not shifting focus on blame or poor performance somewhere else or on others.

Personal Drive – a measurement of how strongly a person feels the need to achieve, accomplish, or complete something.

Personal Relationships – the motivation generated by the importance of forming personal relationships with the people with whom you work.

Persuading Others – the ability to convince others, to present one's viewpoint in such a way that it is accepted by others.

*Planning and Organization – The ability to establish a process for activities that lead to the implementation of systems, procedures, or outcomes.

Practical Thinking – the ability to make practical, common sense decisions; to see and understand what is happening in a common sense way.

Proactive Thinking – the ability to evaluate future implications of current decisions and action; the ability to mentally create the scenarios and outcomes of situations that could develop from decisions or plans of action.

Problem Management – the ability to keep critical issues in context so that you can understand what is happening and effectively use one's knowledge to solve problems.

Problem/Situation Analysis – the ability to identify the elements of a problem situation and to understand which components are critical; the ability to identify critical activities in a process – to be able to break the process down into its component activities.

*Problem Solving Ability – the ability to identify alternative solutions to a problem and to select the best option; the ability to identify the system component that is causing the error, as well as the options available for resolving it and completing the task.

Project and Goal Focus – the ability to maintain your direction in spite of obstacles in your path; the ability to stay on target, regardless of circumstance.

Project Scheduling – the ability to understand the proper allocation of resources for the purpose of getting things done within a defined timeframe.

Quality Orientation – a person's affinity for seeing details, grading them against a pre-set standard, and identifying flaws.

Realistic Expectations – the ability to have expectations of other people that can realistically be met, either in quality of production or quality of performance.

Realistic Goal Setting for Others – the ability to set goals for others that can be achieved using available resources and operating within a projected timeframe; the ability to utilize previous measurable performance in the establishing of goals or quotas.

Realistic Personal Goal Setting – the ability to set goals for yourself that can be achieved using available resources and operating within a projected timeframe.

Relating to Others – the ability to coordinate personal insights and knowledge of others into effective actions; the ability to make use of accurate interpersonal skills in interacting with others.

*Resiliency – The ability to quickly recover from adversity.

Respect for Policies – the ability to see and appreciate the value of conducting business affairs according to the intent of company policies and standards.

Respect for Property – the ability to see and appreciate the value of protecting and correctly using company property.

*Results Orientation – the ability to identify actions necessary to achieve task completion and to obtain results; the ability to meet schedules, deadlines, quotas, and performance goals.

Role Awareness – your ability to see your role in the world, or within a given environment; your ability to understand the expectations placed on a position and to see clearly how those expectations are to be met.

Role Confidence – the ability to develop and maintain an inner strength based on the belief that one will succeed.

Seeing Potential Problems – the ability to structure current situations in an ongoing scenario and identify developments that could cause problems in the future.

Self Assessment – the ability to practically and objectively identify one's personal management strengths and weaknesses; the ability to take the skills and techniques gained in evaluating external situations and apply them to evaluating your own performance and abilities.

Self Confidence – the ability to develop and maintain inner strength based on desire to succeed; a person's belief that he or she possesses the capabilities to succeed.

Self Direction – the internal drive to excel in a chosen career path; a desire to be "better" than you currently are, no matter how good you have already become.

Self Improvement – the motivation that a person has based on the importance of improving oneself; the motivation to obtain training and educational growth opportunities.

*Self Management** – the ability to prioritize and complete tasks in order to deliver desired outcomes within allotted time frames.

*Self-Starting Ability** – the ability to find your own motivation for accomplishing a task, and the degree to which you will maintain this course in the face of adversity.

Sense of Belonging – how motivated a person is by feeling like part of a team or a member of a group.

Sense of Mission – A measure of a person's sense of purpose in his or her Life.

Sense of Self - A measure of a person's awareness of "who" they are – the ability to discern one's own self-worth.

Sense of Timing - the ability to accurately evaluate what is happening in such a way that statements, decisions, and actions are the most effective, accurate, and timely.

Sensitivity to Others – the ability to be sensitive and aware of the feelings of others, but not allow this awareness to get in the way of making objective decisions.

Status and Recognition - A measure of the importance of social status or prestige to a person's current role.

Surrendering Control – the ability to surrender control of a given situation; the ability to be comfortable in a situation where a significant portion of the responsibility for achieving a goal lies in the hands of others.

Systems Judgment – the ability to be balanced in getting things accomplished within the external system of people and things within which you work; your affinity for schematic thinking.

Taking Responsibility – measure of the capacity to be answerable for personal actions.

*Teamwork –The ability to cooperate with others

Theoretical Problem Solving – a person's ability to apply problem solving abilities in a mental, or abstract, scenario; the ability to create, operate, and identify problems in a hypothetical situation, then to manufacture the appropriate response to resolve the problem.

Understanding Attitude – the ability to "read between the lines" in understanding such things as body language, reticence, stress, and emotions.

Understanding Motivational Needs – the ability to understand the needs and desires of employees enough that this knowledge may be used to motivate them to succeed; the ability to encourage a self-starting, active pursuit of goals and objectives.

Using Common Sense – the ability to focus on practical thinking; the ability to see the world clearly.

After identifying your three talents that you would like to improve, add these to your Talents Goal Planning Sheet and ask spirit for the specific action steps that will help you become more talented.

* Represents the top 25 Talents of Mankind

Your Talents Goal Planning Sheet

Goal:

_____

_____

Personal Benefits:

1. _____
2. _____
3. _____
4. _____
5. _____
6. _____
7. _____
8. _____

Action Steps:

1. _____
2. _____
3. _____
4. _____
5. _____
6. _____
7. _____
8. _____
9. _____
10. _____

Chapter 6

Your Beliefs

The word belief is defined in Webster's dictionary as an opinion, conviction, or attitude that one has about something. An attitude is defined as the position we have regarding a person or thing. We all have beliefs or attitudes about everything, but we are usually unaware of many of our own beliefs. As we embrace CMT, we become aware of our current beliefs and then choose which beliefs serve us from our Higher Self, as well as those beliefs that were created by our *"committee"* for our demise.

Beliefs are like the wind. You cannot see them, yet they are the force that alters your current and future conditions about yourself and experiences in your life. Your beliefs about yourself, this world, and God either limit or expand your success and eternal Happiness. The thoughts we have consciously or unconsciously accepted are our beliefs. This is why we must choose our thoughts carefully, for our thoughts and thus beliefs will create our destiny. If you change your thinking, you will change your Life!

Where Our Beliefs Come From

Most of our beliefs have come from sources other than Spirit. We have been brought up with parents, teachers, peers, and society that have taught us what to believe. Most of these beliefs have been accepted with little or no intentional choosing of those thoughts; yet many of these beliefs are not the truth about you or the world you think you live in.

The only valid beliefs are those you have taken the time to contemplate for yourself as guided by the Holy Spirit and then accepted as your own. Through the ages man has believed such things as the world being flat and that man could not fly. We continue to improve our understanding as we know the earth is round and that we can even fly to the moon!

Recognizing and Changing Our Beliefs

There are seven words from Proverbs that shape our world. These are *"As you think, so shall you be."* It does not say as you be, so shall you think. It is written over 2,500 years ago in the Dhammapada that *"We are what we think. All that we are arises with our thoughts.With our thoughts we make the world."* Your freedom lies in your ability to recognize your current beliefs and then change those beliefs that no longer serve you and come from your Source.

Consider what beliefs you have that are preventing you from having the success you want in your Life. Then consider which beliefs you wish to change. As you change your beliefs to the Truth of who you are, you will change your Life and the conditions that you currently live under.

Specifically, consider what you believe to be true about your God and professional goal. Do you believe it can be achieved? If you believe it can be, it will; if you don't, it won't! What obstacles are preventing you from achieving your goals? Consider them and then believe there is a solution. A solution always exists when you believe.

Five Steps To True Beliefs

Are your beliefs true and do they serve you? For those beliefs that do not serve you, ask yourself the following questions:

Step 1: Is your belief the truth?

Step 2: Is your belief the truth for all other people?

Step 3: How do you feel when you think about your belief?

Step 4: How do you feel if you would not have this belief?

Step 5: Now state the opposite of this belief. Which belief is true about you?

For example, if your belief is that you do not have a good memory, is this belief true? Of course NOT! You remember the *"Green Zone!"* A bad memory is not applicable to everyone, why would it be applicable to you? You likely feel inferior with this belief, and would feel good about yourself without it. The restated belief is "I have a good memory," and this is True about you!

Consider these false beliefs you may have and use the 5 step formula to eliminate those that are not the Truth about you:

- ✗ *I am a "night person." Just go to bed one hour earlier!*
- ✗ *I am a "morning person." Just go to bed one hour later!*
- ✗ *Because of the color of my skin I will not be successful. Consider Obama!*
- ✗ *Because I am Hispanic I will not be successful. The wealthiest man in the world today is Hispanic… he recently surpassed Bill Gates!*
- ✗ *I am not good with names. When you meet a person, only focus on their name and repeat their name six times to yourself…you will be great with names!*
- ✗ *I have a bad memory. Mentally focus on the Present Moment and nothing else.*
- ✗ *I am fat, or ugly, or some other false sense of your physical self. Only you believe this and you are perfectly unique!*
- ✗ *I will never have a significant partner because of _____. If you continue to believe this, then you are correct. Eliminate this false belief about yourself.*

Low Pay Off Activities (LPOA's)

Low pay off activities get in your way of achieving your goals. The first *low pay off activity* is your *"committee"* thoughts. These are the red zone thoughts such as f.e.a.r. (false evidence appearing real), worry, and doubt. Continue to monitor your thoughts and let go of any LPOA's. Focus on those thoughts that will lead you to achieving your God, professional, and personal goals.

The second *low pay off activity* is the words you choose that create obstacles to your success. Examples include your responses to "how are you doing?", "how are you feeling?" and "what's going on?" Answers such as "I'm not doing very well," "I don't feel good," and "not much is going on" will create these negative situations and even worse! It has been said the "the poor will get poorer and the rich will get richer." This sounds unjust until we understand that whatever we say to ourselves or each other will give you not only what you say, but more of it! If you have statements that reflect lack and limitation, you will get more of it! The good news is that when you state abundance and Happiness, you will get more of it. Thus, your words that state how well you are doing, how great you feel, and how many wonderful things are in your Life will create that and more for you.

The third *low pay off activity* is your actions. For example, let's say that you plan your day and prioritize five contacts you would need to make to help you achieve your goal. But instead of contacting those key people, you call several people that are "easier" to talk with, yet they don't help you achieve your objectives. This is a low pay off activity that many of us are not even aware of doing every day in both our professional and personal Life.

Creating A Successful Life

Everything is possible for those who believe. This statement does not say some things are possible, or many things are possible. It states everything is possible. History has shown that the person who says "it cannot be done" is usually interrupted by the person who is doing it!

It has been written that anyone can do anything. If you believe this, you have created a miracle mindset for yourself. If you don't believe this, then ask yourself why you don't and change those beliefs that are limiting you.

You can create the Life that you always wanted by intentionally applying the three step process of Conscious Mind Treatment:

Step 1 – The process begins with your thoughts and beliefs that originate from your Godly mind. Good, positive thoughts about you and your success are essential to creating the Life you desire. Being aligned with and guided by the Holy Spirit will create your direction and path. Using visualizations will assist you in creating the pictures in your mind of success.

Visualizations are what you see in your mind's eye and that you will then experience in your Life. Picture yourself achieving your oneness with God and achieving your professional and personal goals simply by asking the Holy Spirit to show you the path to Heaven. See yourself in perfect Peace, Happiness, and Joy! See your goals being achieved in very specific sight, sound, smell, and touch in your mind's eye.

Visualizations have been proven to work. For example, two professional basketball teams were asked to record their average three point completion rate. One team was asked to invest a week practicing three point shots. The other team was asked to sit in a room and visualize shooting three point shots. The team that visualized had a statistically significant improvement over the team that practiced all week, even though that team never touched a basketball!

Most of our creations are stopped in step one. We think of good ideas and then the *"committee"* shoots them down saying things such as "you can't do that,", "that would be impossible to achieve,", and "what would other people think?"! If you do what other people think you should do, that is the action you will take rather than what you have been guided to do. Though we know these statements to ourselves and statements of others are not the path to Truth, we often surrender to the *"committee."* Visualizations will help you overcome the "committee" and enhance your belief in yourself and your amazing ability to do all things.

Step 2 - The next step is to create with the power of your WORDS, as you 'ask and you shall receive.' Know that your words are powerful and create exactly what you state. Be careful with what you say to yourself and others. Using affirmations will help you direct your words.

Affirmations are positive statements that are made in the present tense. The most powerful affirmations and two most important words you can say are *"I AM"* and then end it with whatever you think you are from your Higher Self. For example, if I need to improve my listening skills, my affirmation might be "I am a good listener." Other affirmations could include "I am successful," "I am whole and complete," "I am abundant" and "I am the son of God." To recognize who you really are, use the affirmation "I am Spirit" as this shall treat your mind to the fruit of Life.

When you begin to change your beliefs, make certain that you do not use double negatives. A double negative is when you state that you are NOT (the first negative) something you choose not to be (the second negative). For example, if you wish to stop smoking, your affirmation would not be "I am not inadequate." The explanation is that when you mention "inadequate" your conscious mind and the *"committee"* thinks about being inadequate! To live in the state of your Higher Self, *Conscious Mind Treatment* eliminates any negative thoughts and is filled with Spirit's thoughts in your mind.

We are usually unaware of the power our words have on our Lives. For example, do you believe that you "don't have enough time?" Do you wonder why you don't have enough time? The data shows that if you worked seven days a week, ten hours per day, and slept eight hours each night, you would still have forty-two hours left each week to do whatever you choose! We think we don't have enough time because we have said to ourselves and other people that "I don't have enough time." We all have plenty of time. The only reason why we think we don't is because our word is so powerful that it creates the perception of no time in our Lives. When we say we don't have enough time…we won't. When we say we have all the time in the world, we will!

Step 3 - Through your deed or action, the word is demonstrated in your Life. Act on what you think and say, and this will create what you expect from Life. By acting on one new action step each week, you will be led to the achievement of your goal. Procrastination will lead to a Life of limitation and lack, so just *DO IT*. Don't think any more about it and act on your goals and daily behaviors today.

Change your consciousness to Godly Beliefs, and eliminate those beliefs that no longer serve you. Then combine your thought, word, and deed and you will

literally create the Life that you have always desired.
Enjoy the journey!

Chapter 7

Your "Emotional Intelligence" EQ

Why Emotional Intelligence Is Critical To Your Success

Traits of a person who is led by the Holy Spirit include having a high level of EQ or Emotional Intelligence. In this world, it was thought that a good track record of experience and a deep breadth of training both formal and/or informal created an effective and productive person. Within the past decade, it has been discovered that there is one additional key element that can make your Life and relationships more fulfilling and successful. That element is Emotional Intelligence or EQ.

Research released by the Center for Creative Leadership found that employees who received coaching and training in EQ were three times more likely to succeed than their counterparts who did not. It has also been found that 27 percent of employees hired ultimately failed within two years because of the lack of emotional intelligence. More individuals lost their jobs for lack of emotional intelligence than for poor technical capabilities.

It was also discovered that EQ can help all people become more effective no matter what their job description or title. It can improve all relationships both professionally and personally. Managers who took emotional intelligence training outperformed other divisions in yearly earning goals by 20 percent. Sales organizations increased sales by 11 percent versus other divisions without emotional intelligence training, and retention increased by over 20 percent with EQ training.

In a recent survey of business executives, three driving forces of competitive advantage were identified. They are: building trusting relationships, increasing energy and effectiveness under pressure, and creating the future. Emotional intelligence can help build these as well as other areas of your Life.

Defining Emotional Intelligence

Emotional intelligence is one's capability to work well with others and respond to environmental pressures and demands appropriately. It is the ability to sense, understand and effectively apply the power of emotions and mental clarity as a source of human energy, information, connection and influence. Emotional Intelligence is about your personal mastery between "reason and intuition" and "head to heart."

CMT includes the mental awareness of yourself and others. The six components of emotional intelligence are: emotional self-awareness, emotional expression to others, emotional awareness of others, intentional creativity, compassion, and intuition.

Emotional Self-Awareness

Emotional self-awareness is the degree to which you are aware of your feelings, identify what those feelings are, and then connect to their source. Emotions are feelings or "gut-level" instincts or reactions. Unlike thoughts, they are not cognitive but are sensed or experienced. Ask yourself how attuned you are to your feelings, how able you are to identify where they come from, and do you believe in them. Self-Awareness allows you to use emotions as a valuable insight about yourself, others, and the events and situations around you.

Begin to notice your emotional state and the source of your emotions. If you are sitting up straight and feeling great, try to determine the reason. Ask yourself: "Do you like the people you are with?", "Do you like your environment?" and "Are you thinking about your feelings of confidence and security?". Understand the source of your feelings. Connect your feelings to the person, issue, situation, or concern, and then expand your vocabulary to better describe your emotional state. Ask yourself, "Can I name my feelings and am I aware of my feelings?" Rank your feelings on a continuum from mild to strong and place different words at different points on that continuum. You may be filled with joy, moderately confident, or somewhat happy.

Emotional Expression To Others

Emotional expression is the degree to which you can express your feelings to others, verbalizing your emotions in such a way that the information is placed into Godly and productive use. For example, when you are talking to someone and you sense they are not listening, you may pause and ask that person if they are "still with you." Focus on positive emotional expression with others, practicing enthusiasm and appreciation. This is how you can "shine your light" on other people. The beauty is that as you shine positive emotional expression, you will get back more positive emotional expression from others. Begin to express your feelings on a daily basis to others and, at least once per day, express your appreciation to another person. You can track this behavior on your *1-31 Tracking Sheet.*

Emotional Awareness Of Others

Emotional awareness of others is the ability to hear, sense, and intuit (or be independent of any reasoning process) what other people may be feeling, from their body language, tone of voice, or words. Most people speak about 120 words per minute, yet your mind runs at 400-600 words per minute. Since you have this "extra time" use it to listen to what the person is saying while also considering their emotional energy, their mood, and the types of emotional words they use. These words may include "I am worried," "I am concerned," "I am happy to report," or "I feel." Ask yourself "how is this person feeling right now?" An effective affirmation to increase your emotional awareness of others is to say "I am an effective listener" implying that you are also listening to the emotional content of their words.

Intentional Creativity

To be intentional and live in the Green Zone, we must better manage distractions, remain focused on our goals, and be consistent in bringing about events that will help us reach our goals. Before you enter into the next activity ask yourself: "what do I want to have happen here?" and "what are my feelings telling me?"

Creativity is the ability to tap multiple non-cognitive resources that will allow you to envision powerful new ideas, frame alternative solutions, and find effective new ways of doing things. Know that there is always a better idea and solution to any obstacle you have in your Life.

At Microsoft, people will meet and have an intense brainstorming session. They will then leave and go meditate and clear their minds. Afterwards, when they are not thinking of the challenge, new ideas begin to blossom. Another way to be creative is to think about contradictory ideas, or develop visualizations of the end results. In an intentional, peaceful, and STILL state of mind, ask yourself: "what is another idea that will help me achieve my goal?"

Compassion

Compassion is the ability to forgive, Love and honor yourself and others. To be compassionate is to not only "walk in another's shoes" but it is about "being that other person." If each of us could literally understand the other person's background, past experiences, beliefs, and point of view, we would never have conflict for we would compassionately understand them. Believe that each person is doing the best he can, and you will have the compassion necessary to have wonderful relationships with all people.

A very simple, but not easy, method to show others compassion is to not judge. It has been said that 'judge not that ye be not judged' and the 'measure of judgment you give shall be measured against you.' Judging is only a reflection of your own understanding, or better states the reflection of your lack of understanding. To recognize the difference between judging and having an opinion, look at your emotions. If you are emotional about your opinion of another, you are judging another. Forgive yourself and forgive others and know that all people are good. Then go beyond forgiving and ask yourself "How can I serve this person?"

Intuition

Intuition is about following Spirit and your heart. It is the degree to which you notice, trust, and actively use your hunches, gut-level reactions, senses and other non-cognitive responses that are produced by your senses, emotion, and body.

Have you even known you were right about something, though you didn't know the reasons why? Can you see the finished product before it is complete and without a path? Do you believe in your dreams even when others cannot see or understand them? If so, you are in tune with your intuition.

There is a small and quiet voice of Spirit that is always directing you... if you listen to It. Your body and feelings are constantly telling you things. To turn up your volume to this creative intelligence, "check-in" and ask Yourself "what is the right decision?", "how do I feel about this action or decision?", and pause and do your breathing exercise. Turn away from de-valuing your intuition, and instead know that the most innovative and creative solutions lie where your intuition meets your logic.

The Secret To True Emotional Intelligence

All intelligence comes from one Source and that is God. The six emotional intelligence components all come from this Essence, and you can create the type of EQ that is whole and good for you and all of mankind. When keeping "The God Goal" at the top of your mind, you can recognize your Oneness with God, be guided by the Holy Spirit, and have the perfect Emotional Intelligence.

Instead of emotionally responding or reacting to situations, change your consciousness by first establishing your Godly EQ of eternal Peace, oneness with all, stillness, and Joy. As you are guided by the Holy Spirit, asking for your Godly EQ to be ever-present, you will have the perfect EQ within yourself and to all others.

Our EQ has been distorted as we have been led by our ego, also now known as the "committee." We have "committee" emotions of mistrust, f.e.a.r., anger, insecurity, and a host of other "committee" members that are not the Truth of who we really are. Our True and Greater Self only knows the Godly emotional intelligence of trust, Love, security, Happiness, Joy, and Peace. This Truth can only be found within each one of us, and can be simply accessed by asking!

Ask the Holy Spirit to guide you to your True emotional intelligence, and then ask to demonstrate this throughout the day with yourself and with all those you come in contact. To be guided, you merely need to be STILL, quiet your mind, and listen with your mind, heart, and emotions. 'Ask and you shall receive,' knock and the door shall open, 'seek and you shall findeth.'

As you are guided by the Holy Spirit, your emotional intelligence will enhance your Life as your relationship with yourself shall blossom, along with your relationships with all others. EQ provides you the tools to increase your effectiveness under all situations and conditions. The pressure of any situation shall evaporate as you build trusting and loving relationships with yourself and others, creating the future you have always known is your inheritance.

To evaluate your EQ, complete the *EQ survey* questions honestly. Scores of 11-12 in each section is optimal, 9-10 is proficient, 7-8 is vulnerable and 6 or below is a caution. Begin to develop the areas of EQ that you determine to be most beneficial to you. Though your behavioral style and values typically do not change, you can increase your EQ as you mentally focus to improve these areas.

Your Emotional Quotient (EQ) Assessment

Directions: For the items listed below, indicate how well it describes the way you currently think or feel about yourself. (3) = Very much; (2) = Moderately; (1) = A little; (0) = Not at all

Emotional Self-Awareness

	YES			NO
- I can put words behind my feelings	3	2	1	0
- I listen to my feelings	3	2	1	0
- I am aware of my feelings	3	2	1	0
- I accept my feelings as my own	3	2	1	0

Emotional Expression to Others

	YES			NO
- I let others know how I feel	3	2	1	0
- I tell others when they excel	3	2	1	0
- I express my positive emotions	3	2	1	0
- I I express my negative emotions	3	2	1	0

Emotional Awareness of Others

	YES			NO
- I can recognize emotions in others	3	2	1	0
- I am always a good listener	3	2	1	0
- I sense others unspoken feelings	3	2	1	0
- I can "read between the lines"	3	2	1	0

Intentional Creativity

	YES			NO
- I finish things that I start	3	2	1	0
- I know how to say "no" to others	3	2	1	0
- I visualize the future	3	2	1	0
- I get excited about new ideas	3	2	1	0

Compassion

	YES			NO
- I am ethical with others	3	2	1	0
- I can "be" the other person	3	2	1	0
- I happily help other people	3	2	1	0
- I enjoy seeing others be successful	3	2	1	0

Intuition

	YES			NO
- I trust in my hunches	3	2	1	0
- I listen to the soft voice within me	3	2	1	0
- I use intuition/logic to make decisions	3	2	1	0
- I believe in my dreams and visions	3	2	1	0

Chapter 8

Prioritizing Your Life

Though we are not from this world, we are of this world and that includes time. Each one of us has the same amount of time that can be effective increased with CMT. We can't borrow time, hoard time, save time, or even steal time. However, we can maximize our time through scheduling and planning. Effective scheduling and planning of our time will help determine your success.

Monthly Planning

The upcoming month is the only month of this year that you will ever be given, so let's make the most of it! It usually takes about two hours to plan your month, and should be completed the last weekend of the previous month. This includes developing your Mission and Purpose, Personal Goals to focus on this month, Business Goals to focus on this month, and prioritizing these goals.

Your Mission and Purpose

If you do not know what your mission and purpose is in Life, you will never get there! Consider now what your relationship is with God, and how you want to be to yourself and your fellow man. This may include things such as always being led by the Holy Spirit, the best spouse, the best employee, to own a company, to become independently wealthy, or to serve others. As you contemplate your mission each month you will begin to develop the statement that aligns with God's Will.

An example of a Mission and Purpose Statement is: "To recognize my oneness with God every Holy Instant, while helping myself and others become our greatest possibility." You are already experiencing success with your mission in Life as you focus each month on what you want to become. Write down your Mission/Purpose on the *"Monthly Planning Form."*

Monthly Planning Sheet

Mission/Purpose

Prioritize **Top Personal and Business Goals:**

Prioritize **Personal Goals To Focus On This Month:**

Family/Home

Financial/Career

Mental/Educational

Physical/Health

Social/Cultural

Spiritual/Ethical

Prioritize **High Payoff Activities:**

TARGET DATE | **Imperative Project List**

TARGET DATE | **Important Project List**

Prioritize **Business Goals To Focus On This Month:**

* Transfer your High Priority Goals to the Top Personal and Business Goals Section.

Personal Goals To Focus On This Month

Your Life is more than your work. If you only focus on work you will wake up one day wondering why you aren't happy and where all your loved ones went. To ensure your long-term success, a balanced Life is required in the six areas outlined below. As you go through each area of your Life, write down your thoughts on how you are going to consciously focus this month on improving them. Ask the Holy Spirit to guide you through this process.

Spiritual – Ask yourself what you will do this month to strengthen your recognition of your Oneness with God. These goals may include the daily tracking of your conscious time invested with God and your Oneness with Him, or meditating each morning and night as you become quiet and STILL both mentally and physically. As your spirituality is connected as One with all people, another action step may include the daily consciousness to honor all those you are in contact.

Family and Loved Ones – Ask: "what can I do this month to have an even stronger Love relationship with my family and loved ones?" Review your month and determine who you will intentionally encourage and Love, noting holidays and birthdays that you can now make the most of. This may include planning a family picnic, investing time with each child or your significant other each day, or an extraordinary gesture you will do with them each week. Whatever your intention, write it down and schedule the activities for the month.

Financial and Career – You will never be in a position to retire and do something else that you were gifted and blessed with, unless you plan for it. Determine your financial and career goals and then identify what you will do this month to achieve them. Your goal may include being financially independent in ten years, and your monthly action steps may include tracking your spending each day, determining how much you can save this month, seeing a financial advisor, and sharing your goal with loved ones while asking them for help to achieve your goal. None of us are successful without other people helping us in all areas of our Life.

Mental and Educational - What you put into your mind is what you think about and what ultimately comes out in your words and actions. Do you recognize daily your oneness with God? Do you read one book per month, subscribe to your industry's trade magazine, or listen to self-help tapes? For this upcoming month, identify what you are going to put into your mind and your thoughts, words, and deeds will be Godly.

Physical and Health – Our bodies are used for communicating our oneness with God and each other. What new behavior do you want to develop this month that will further improve your health? You may want to do daily deep breathing exercises each day, walking three times a week, drinking 8 glasses of water a day, seeing your doctor for a physical this month, or having a healthy breakfast each day. Whatever your intention, write what activity you will begin this month to improve your physical and mental health to better serve God, yourself, and others.

Social and Cultural – You have been blessed with many wonderful things that may include your good health, a wonderful job with a great company, and a loving family. The question is what are you giving back to God, yourself, family, company, church, charity or society? Your giving back may be as simple as being a friendly neighbor, or when meeting a person you honor them and consider them a friend, not a stranger. There is a universal law that states whatever you give, you will receive back ten-fold. Ask yourself what you are going to give back this month to enrich your Life and the Life of others.

Business Goals To Focus On This Month

This monthly planning section is dedicated to developing the business goals that will help you achieve your professional goal. This could include being intentional with your clients, or team by recognizing and complementing them, or identifying a project that will create value for the organization and your customers. Ask yourself "What can I do this month that will help me achieve my business goals?" Then write down your thoughts on the *"Monthly Planning Form."*

Your Top Personal and Business Goals

We can't do all the things we would like to next month. Once you have been STILL and asked to be guided on the things you should focus on next month with your professional and personal goals, prioritize which are most important. Write down these prioritized goals and begin to achieve them by scheduling time in your time management system to track your accomplishments. This process will help you achieve a balanced, successful, and Godly Life.

Delegate, Eliminate, Simplify, and Communicate (DESC)

Earlier you were asked to identify how much time you were investing in your *"High Pay Off Activities"* (HPOA's), and how much time you were spending in your *"Low Pay Off Activities"* (LPOA's). To increase the amount of time you invest in your HPOA's, we must decrease our LPOA's by delegating, simplifying, and communicating with others.

Delegate – Most anything that you do can be done by others through training. Our "committee" steers us into false ideas such as "I can do it faster" and it "takes too much time to train them." Identify those activities that must be done but can be done by someone else. This may be delegated to a peer, subordinate, assistant, friend, your child, or even the boss!

Eliminate – We do some activities out of habit. Review all your activities, determine which ones are no longer necessary and eliminate them. If you are not sure if you need them, try a day, week, or month of not doing them and see if it negatively affects the business or if anyone even notices!

Simplify – Other low pay off activities can be simplified. You may no longer have a need to go through a long approval process, or you could automate some of the processes to streamline your operation and everyday schedule.

Communicate – If nothing else, you can ask your team members, family, clients, or any internal or external customers what suggestions they may have to improve your effectiveness. They will be more willing to help when you provide a benefit they will receive from doing this. Benefits could include providing faster service with higher quality, or having less stress with more success in your work place or home Life.

Managing Interruptions

For the next three days record all interruptions that you encounter. These interruptions could be a mix of people, emails, faxes, and telephone calls. Record each type of interruption and the cause of the interruptions. There are some productive interruptions, though most are not necessary.

For example, you will find that there are a handful of people that regularly interrupt you during the day. Once you identify your key interrupters, set an appointment to discuss these interruptions and the negative impact that they have on everyone's time. Do not confront an interrupter at the time of the interruption as they will typically react in a defensive manner. Instead, meet with them and share ideas on how you can work more effectively together. One solution is to write down the topics for discussion and then meet twice a day to discuss. Some interruptions are timely and necessary, though these are the exceptions once you manage your interrupters. Agreeing on what situations call for immediate interruptions will be helpful to all.

Your Interruptions Worksheet

INTERRUPTER'S NAME	CAUSE FOR THE INTERRUPTION

KEY INTERRUPTERS	KEY CAUSES

Having A Closed Door With An Open Door Policy

Closing your door or facing your desk away from the entrance to your workspace are excellent ways to "give a hint" to others that you do not want to be disturbed. To have an open door policy, let your team know when you will be available to talk with them. This may be a specific time each day or certain days and time of the week. You may also want to post your daily, weekly, or monthly calendar outside of your work space.

Learning To Say "No" In A Nice Way

To manage our Lives we must learn how to manage other people. Saying "No" to another's request can be done by making statements such as: "I have another commitment right now, could we schedule a time to meet later in the day?", or "Let me train you how to do this and then you won't need to wait for me," or "The person you need to speak with is Susan as she can help you better than I can about that topic." Practice saying "No" in a nice way and you will find that it saves both you and the other person time that can then be invested in HPOA's.

Since we all have the same amount of time, your success will depend on your effective and relentless use of planning, scheduling, and prioritizing your Life.

Your monthly planning and focus on increasing your time invested in HPOA's will pay dividends in the form of even more success in your Life.

Chapter 9

Treating the Subconscious Mind

In addition to treating the Conscious Mind, there is a new technology where we can bypass the *"critical factor"* of our conscious mind and establish Godly selective thinking utilizing new thought patterns. This technology is referred to as *"Subconscious Mind Treatment"* or "SMT." Understanding the mind and the *"Critical Factor"* allows us to change our beliefs to recognize our sinlessness, Holiness and Oneness with God. Below is an analysis of the three levels of the mind and how Life works:

The Three Levels of the Mind

Level 1: The "Unconscious Mind" is programmed to operate automatic bodily functions. Heart rate, blood pressure, pupil dilation, digestion of food, hair growth and all the other body functions that you don't have to think of for them to happen are handled by this portion of our minds. This part of the mind is critical to live in our bodies, but not critical to understand the Truth about who we really are.

Level 2: The "Conscious Mind" is where you process all the thoughts you have at the present moment. You are aware of these thoughts. It is very rational and analytical using the *Critical Factor* of the conscious mind. The *Critical Factor* is the watch guard over information that comes to you from the outside world and protects information you have stored in the subconscious mind. The *Critical Factor* decides which information will be allowed and passed into the subconscious mind. For example, let's say that you are holding a water bottle in your right hand and someone comes and tells you that you are holding the water bottle with your left hand. Your *Critical Factor* checks your beliefs and in this case confirms that you are indeed holding the bottle in your right hand. This is an important function of the mind. Without it we would constantly change our beliefs as new information is received. This is why pure conscious thought is unable to make lasting changes and the old beliefs remain for a Life time, even when these beliefs work against us. Keeping these same beliefs that no longer serve us, we will find ourselves right back to where started from. When bypassing the *Critical Factor*, we can change our beliefs and subconscious mind, allowing us to be free from bondage of beliefs that no longer serve us.

Establishment of acceptable selective thinking is your willingness to accept new thoughts with the *"Critical Factor"* of your mind and provide new beliefs that lead to The Path of Peace, Happiness, Joy, and success in your Life.

Level 3: The "Subconscious Mind" is where your mind holds beliefs and where habit patterns take place. This is where we create new thought patterns and create positive beliefs to become successful. By accepting positive ideas in this level of the mind creates lasting changes.

To dissolve the *Critical Factor* one must be STILL, relax, and become quiet with our mind, feelings, and body. As you become STILL you become aware of the Holy Spirit that will lead you to the Truth about you, and lead you to your Source. To achieve this state of complete enlightenment, do the following:

Allow your mind to become comfortable and relaxed, opening your mind to new possibilities and information. Close your eyes and quiet your mind, allowing your body and mind to become STILL. Closing your eyes helps to shut out the outside world and open your inside world. Say to yourself "relax" and breathe deeply, mentally focusing on your breathing and being in the state of relaxation. As you relax with long, slow breathing tell yourself that you are going deeper and deeper within your essence. Now visualize a small flame within you. This is the Light of God within all of us.

Focus on this small Light within and watch It as It grows larger within you. Your Light begins to move throughout your body and mind. Feel It seep out of all the pores of your body. Your Light begins to surround you and provides a Halo around you, protecting you always, giving you only Heavenly thoughts, with angels dancing and singing around you.

Your Light now goes out into the room and then beyond, touching all those you Love extending to all your Brothers and Sisters. In this enlightened state you now recognize your Oneness with God and ask to be led into the warm embrace of your Creator. Lay here in your eternal Peace, Happiness, and Joy, knowing this is the True perception of your Holy Self.

As you place yourself in this state of Truth your subconscious and conscious mind will become One with each Present Moment of your Eternal Life. The more often you do this the more you shall hear the "Voice of God" and recognize your eternal safety and how each Moment is a state of Gratitude, Peace, Love, and Joy. This understanding of SMT can then be used to have Life work for you!

"We walk in the dark and each of us must learn to turn on his, or her, own Light." Earl Nightingale

How Life Works

We no longer need to live in hell here on earth. No longer need we ask for anything from God, for He has already given us all we will ever need. Within each one of us is God's Peace and Joy and all I need to do is go within myself and ask the Holy Spirit to guide me to the Holy Place. Once in this place of Peace, Life shall work with me, no longer against me.

Life then is managed by me, with God, in three phases:

All Life first works with your Conscious Mind. This is "first thought" where when joined with God you have a Godly conscious thought. An example might be having the thought of what should I do for income to serve and be the Light of the world. In spiritual terms, when considering the Father, Son, and Holy Ghost, this Conscious thought would be the Father. This is also considered the SEED of creation where you are involved in the sowing process.

The path from your Conscious Mind to your Subconscious Mind can be freed by allowing your "Critical Factor" and CMT to allow a free flow of Godly thoughts to sink into your Subconscious Mind. Most of us have many "weeds" that prevent us from having Life work for us instead of against us. CMT is the means to put "weed killer" on your path from the *Conscious* to *Subconscious Mind*.

This conscious thought or "seed thought" sinks into your Subconscious mind with CMT. The Subconscious then begins to develop the perfect answer or solution of your conscious thought. We have been given free choice and any thought you have will be developed by your Subconscious mind. The subconscious works by acting on "your wish is my command." The "wish" is your thought of what you seek. In spiritual terms this is the Holy Ghost and is considered to be the rich fertile soil where the seed grows. Many are unable to create fluidly as the condition of their soil is filled with weeds from the *"committee!"*

The third phase is experiencing the results of your thought and the creation of the thought by your subconscious. These results become your experience, or your harvest, after the sowing. In spiritual terms this is considered the Son, as Christ experienced Life on earth. Your experience will either land you in Heaven or hell, depending upon your Conscious thoughts and if they were jointly created or created by your lower self.

Conscious Mind Treatment Process

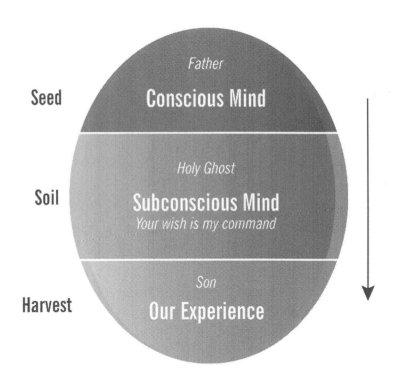

Chapter 10

CMT Thoughts That Lead To Peace and Success

There are critical thoughts in CMT that can change your Life and lead you to God and success in the world. Most of us do not accept new ideas until at least the sixth time. You would benefit by reviewing these ideas at least six times, in a state of Oneness and Light as described in Chapter 9, to fully embrace their meaning and Truth.

You Are Spirit, Not Your Body

The first thought change is to recognize that you are not your body. Ultimately, we are Spirit! We have been exposed to so many thoughts about our body controlling us, versus our mind controlling our body that we have lost the Truth about who we are. We are not a body, for it is self-evident that the body eventually dies, goes to ashes and is not everlasting. We are not a prisoner within a body in a world where things appear to live then appear to die. When we maintain the laws the world obeys, we see our frailties. We perceive sins as real and inescapable, bringing f.e.a.r. to us. When bound this way, we do not know our Father or ourselves. But we are everlasting and the body is simply a means of communication while here on earth. Only when we recognize our oneness with God and are led by the Holy Spirit does our body become Holy. Let us stop having our bodies run us and instead have our mind and spirit manage our bodies to do God's work.

Each morning say "I am not my body, I am Spirit." Each time you think you experience bodily pain, say "I am not my body, I am Spirit." Rise above your physical self by asking the Holy Spirit to help you, and go within where your Spirit and Godly mind rest. Be still and experience Heaven right here on earth.

Today is the day to declare your freedom, no longer are you a prisoner within a body, and no longer are you bound to the laws of the world where frailties and sins are perceived as real with no escape. Your Truth is free, and what is bound is not part of Truth. God's Son is free, as his Father is free and given His Son Freedom. Once you believe you are not your body and not from this world, you can rise above your smaller self and know you are everlasting spirit. After you say "I am not my body," declare who you are…"I am Spirit!"

Do Not Attack

The second thought change is to not attack anyone or anything. Whenever you attack anything, you are attacking yourself! We all come from the same Source and we are all one with each other. Every thought of attack that you have takes you further away from God, and further away from your worldly success.

Attack takes many forms. We attack others when they do not have the same beliefs as we do. We attack ideas that appear to jeopardize our safety. Our attack separates us from everything to include ourselves. We become confused, frustrated, and our Life makes no sense.

Replace attack thoughts with thoughts of oneness and acceptance. When another attacks you, do not attack back. Instead look at that person as they are - one with you coming from the same Source. No one can hurt you eternally and it is useless to acknowledge or give power to the smaller self of others.

Understanding Forgiveness

Forgiveness is to see with the Eyes of Christ. We typically think of forgiveness as how we forgive another. Seeing the world with the Eyes of God, we see a world of Oneness, Goodness, and Love, with no need to forgive yourself or another. As we see with spirit our sight from our physical eyes will serve us to see the Truth. Without Spirit, and only using our smaller self, we shall make our little judgments and then perceive the world to be made up of what we have inaccurately judged. With Spirit we look upon a liberated world, set free from all judgments, to behold a world with only Love as our gaze is filled with forgiveness.

The 'Second Coming' is when we are in the mental state of forgiveness and CMT, reestablishing the Truth as we allow forgiveness to rest upon all things. This state holds one safe within God's gentle grasp. As forgiveness is realized, the 'Second Coming' returns us to Spirit in the name of our Source and the Will of God.

We join together in Oneness in the Holy Light and clearly see our Father's Love. Simply ask that you abandon your small self and world, and see God's world instead. A world where our Higher Self is revealed and recognized as One with our Father.

The Past Is Dead, The Present Moment Is Bliss

The past is a distorted perception of our thinking and shackles us in chains, preventing our freedom to Love and to be loved. Past thoughts take us to hell wherein lies regret, guilt, shame, and further ideas that lead to jealously, hate, and pain. None of this is the truth about you!

If you are STILL and enjoy right now, the present moment, the past is dead. Our future is only an extension of the present moment. Flow with Life and flow with the Present Moment and you shall experience Bliss.

No Longer Do I Deceive Myself

I have indeed misunderstood the world and deceived myself. I laid my personal perceptions upon the world and saw it as evil. How fierce it seemed. And how deceived was I to think that what I feared was this world, instead of my own mind alone creating hell here on earth. No longer do I deceive myself on who I am or allow the "committee" of tiny thoughts to enter my Peace and paradise.

I Am A Child Of God

Recognize that you, too, are a Child of God. The bible states that you are the child of God. A child of God is the Son of God. When Christ taught us how to pray, His prayer that we call "The Lord's Prayer" begins with 'Our Father.' Not just Christ's Father, but all of us have the same Father. The only difference between Christ and each of us is that Christ had the awareness that He and His Father are One. For most of us, we need the help of Christ and that's why the Bible says to pray 'In Christ's Name.' We need the help of the Holy Spirit, and we need the help of our fellow man.

To not think you are a Child of God is to operate from your lower self, abandoning the responsibility that each of us have to do God's Will. And what is God's Will? Quite simply, for us to recognize our oneness with the Father and to live in Heaven, even here on earth!

The Word Of God

God created us in His own image and likeness. The Word of God is God's thought by Itself that created us by stating 'I create my Son pure and holy as Myself.' This thought made God our Father of the Son He Loves. From that instant of creation, God now creates with us as we are one with the Father. There are no other Words of God from that point on as the World of God is the creation of us that is holy and pure as God Himself.

Heaven Is Not A Place

The fourth thought change is to recognize that Heaven is not a place, but rather Heaven is a state of consciousness as you recognize your Oneness with God. It is amusing to see athletes pointing up when they do well in a sport. They actually should be pointing at themselves, within themselves. Heaven is not a distant place up in the sky. Heaven is always within you. Know that this is true, quiet your mind and ask for Heaven to be felt within you.

Step Back

In all things, step back and let the Holy Spirit guide you. STEP BACK with your thoughts, responses to situations, and responses to others. A means to step back is to slowly count to ten with any thought or response to Life. This will allow you to observe your thoughts, to honor all people, and honor all situations, while allowing spirit to guide you with the appropriate thought or response.

Detach From The World

Nothing in this world is permanent as it goes from dust to dust. Being attached to the world causes us to live Life on a roller coaster of death, disappointment, and misery. By detaching yourself from this world, you will have an ever-increasing Life filled with Peace, Happiness, and Joy. The world is unpredictable, with no guarantees of the future.

Surely disappointment will follow you. Detach from the world and go within yourself where the only sure, steady, constant, and True Peace reside.

I Rule My Destiny

Recognize the fact that "I rule my destiny." It is impossible for anything to come to you that you do not welcome. What happens to you is your desire. We have each been given the freedom of choice. God has given us this freedom of choice, as evidenced by the fact that we are separated from God with our lower consciousness. When you accept the fact that you rule your own destiny, you are led beyond this world to God where your Higher Self resides. Our perception follows our judgment and we therefore see what we look upon. As you rule your destiny, so shall you look upon a destined person.

You are not a victim of Life. You are where you place yourself. Through your conscious mental focus to rule your Life, it shall be done unto you. Each morning awake and state that "I Rule My Destiny" and ask the Holy Spirit to take you to the lawns of Heaven.

The Need For "US"

There are only a few who have reached Heaven by themselves. Christ is one that has reached the

"Heaven Consciousness" and He is willing to guide us. It is the reason that the Bible states to 'Pray in Christ's Name.' For most of "US" to reach the lawns of Heaven, we need each other to both reach the lawns and enter the gates of Heaven. We are all one with each other and we can help each other reach the state of consciousness called "Heaven."

Heaven is not a place; It is a state of Consciousness. Heaven is not a place we physically go to, rather Heaven is a state of mind that can be achieved instantly, or as long you deem necessary! We need nothing but the Truth, as we sought many things and ultimately found death. Now we seek from within us, not from this world, to our final destination.

To reach this destination we need each other for Love and support. Mother Teresa's words of wisdom echo this cry as she shared "Let no one ever come to you without leaving better and happier." It is done unto you as you do unto others. As you attack another, so you attack yourself. However, as you Love another, so you Love yourself. "Love one another" was not just a nice thought; it is a necessity if you wish to have eternal Peace and Happiness.

The need for "US" is developed through intentional reflection of our relationships, ensuring that your relationships touch your peers - those younger than us, and those older than us who typically possess more wisdom. To begin this process, write down the list of people where you have frequent interaction within each of these three categories.

Mentor & Mentee Relationships

Youth	Peers	Elderly

The Youth category can include any people younger than you and should include children as we can learn from them and their innocence, helping you to recognize your oneness with God and 'to come to Me as children.' The ages would include a newborn to 25 years old, and your primary role is to be a mentor to these mentees.

Your peers can include people you work with, your social friends, and within five to ten years of your age, or from ages 25 to 55.

The elderly are those five years older than you and typically fall into the age group from 55 and older. These people should be considered your mentors, with you the mentee.

Review this list and ensure that you have at least three solid relationships in each category. Intentionally identify people that you would like to either begin or further develop a relationship, and list these people along with specific steps to enhance these relationships on the following form.

Mentor & Mentee Action Steps

Category	Name	Action Steps To Develop Relationship
Youth		
Peers		
Elderly		

Act upon the steps you have identified to enhance these relationships. This process will help you understand the value of each age and category, while helping you recognize the need for "US."

Today be present with the Voice for God that speaks an ancient lesson, timeless, changeless, no more today than any day. Seek to hear and learn and understand as you are led by the Holy Spirit. This Voice for God is not heard until we understand that we will hear not alone or apart, but as One together making all things protected for us. We need not be anxious over anything, for His Voice will tell us what to think, to whom to speak, what to say, and where to go.

Recognize Your Oneness With God and Each Other Every Present Moment

We are all one with that same Source, and that Source is God. To have everlasting Peace, Happiness, and Joy, all we need do is recognize our oneness with God each day. Each morning and evening still your mind and ask the Holy Spirit to move you to the Peace within you and to recognize your oneness with God. Here you will have no wants or needs and you will remember who you really are, one with God. Instantly or within a few days, as it is your choice on how long you believe it will take, you shall plant yourself in heaven and have a glorious day each day for eternity.

Today, expect only the happy thing of God to come to you. Simply ask for them to come, and your invitation will be answered by the thoughts to which is has been sent by you. Gently do all things now, fall into place as you accept your Holiness. As we are one in God, all choices are already made, all conflicts are resolved, and everything already given you. Peace is achieved with your heart quiet and your mind at rest.

As you call upon the Holy Spirit in the morning, ask the Holy Spirit to guide you throughout the day. You shall be gently reminded of the Holy Spirit's presence during your day as when we ask we shall always receive. When we seek, we shall always find. When we knock, the door of heaven shall open for all of us. AMEN.

I Sit At The Altar of God

What I see in this world and in my fellow man is merely what I wish to see and it stands for what I want as the truth. To this false perception alone do I respond no matter how impelled I am by the outside world. I choose to see what I would look upon, and this becomes my false perception.

True perception is achieved by going within as I see me as sinless along with my sinless brother. As the red curtain of the *"committee"* is swept away, what stands before me is the altar of Truth. The Light of God now shines into my Mind and it is here, and only here, where my Peace of mind is restored and where I sit at the altar of God!

Further Knowledge

To download forms and for additional information go to www.ConsciousMindTreatment.com

Use Discount Code CMTBOOK

You will have access to all the tools used by Dr. Hank Seitz in his *Conscious Mind Treatment Process* such as:

CMT Behavioral Profile – The *"Conscious Mind Treatment Behavioral Profile"* helps you understanding yourself and others by understanding mankind's Behavioral Styles, removing judgment of others and replaces your thoughts with understanding. Hippocrates had identified four primary behavioral styles of mankind and you now have an opportunity to know your behavioral style by taking the Behavioral Profile and having your own personalized report about you!

CMT Motivation Profile – The Motivational Profile helps you better understand yourself and other people are motivated and how they make decisions. It answers questions such as what is the source of my desire to take action or not! The *"CMT Motivational Profile"* helps you understand why you and others make certain decisions while helping yourself 'speak the language of others', thereby opening the shade of communication and building stronger relationships.

CMT Talents Profile - Measures your 67 Talents to the tenth of a percent using the world's most statistically accurate and valid diagnostic tool to measure your Talents. The results of your Talents profile will help you understand your highest talents to leverage these talents to better serve the world and find your inheritance of wealth and abundance.

CMT Emotional Intelligence Profile - Emotional Intelligence is more critical than your IQ (Intelligence Quotient) and has been found to help you make better decisions. This assessment measures your emotional intelligence and provides your Emotional Quotient score based on your self-awareness, self-regulation, passions, social skills and empathy.

CMT Time Management System - This complete one year time management system is the most comprehensive means to daily improve your conscious mind to create good and rid yourself of the 'committee'. The multi-faceted system goes beyond making appointments and leads you to a fuller and more intentional Life.

About Dr. Hank Seitz

Dr. Hank has a time proven process that guarantees specific and measurable business improvements. He was a General Manager with Procter & Gamble (P&G) for 15 years, managing a billion dollar business in the Southeast United States. At the time, P&G's

patents were running out and they were losing market share, sales, and profits. Dr. Hank decided to develop a process and used this process with Procter & Gamble. The results were astounding as sales grew by 21%, and costs dropped by 34% in less than a year. In addition, all participants improved their personal lives in the process!

He left P&G and began his own practice, with his first client being P&G. Since then he has worked with Coca-Cola, John Deere, IBM, Chase Bank, and 1,000's of other large and small companies in North America that have all achieved bottom line business results.   Dr. Hank specializes in Business Teams, Executives, and Entrepreneurs that are seeking to improve their business results using his time-proven process for the past 15 years.

Credentials: Dr. Hank Seitz is an International Speaker, Author, and works with Business Teams to measurably increase their business results. He has his undergraduate degree in Business from the University of Wisconsin - Madison, Master's Degree in Human Behavior, and PhD in Mental Science. He was a General Manager with Procter & Gamble for 15 years, and for the past 15 years he has used his time proven process with hundreds of Corporations and thousands of business teams. Dr. Hank is a Mental Scientist, Behavioral Psychologist and Business Man.

Business Guarantee: If you do not measurably increase your specific and measurable business results, and receive at least a 400% return on your investment, your investment is returned in full. To attend Dr. Hank's *"Conscious Mind Treatment"* time-proven process that guarantees to measurably increase specific business results contact CMT@GMResults.com

Dr. Hank conducts Personalized Coaching by contacting CMT@GMResults.com

Dr. Hank is available to speak in front of your organization or business by contacting CMT@GMResults.com

Dr. Hank holds workshops on Conscious Mind Treatment and Business Productivity by contacting CMT@GMResults.com

For more information on Dr. Hank and his company Guaranteed Measurable Results, LLC visit www.GMResults.com

9680826R0008

Made in the USA
Charleston, SC
02 October 2011